CW01454637

Southern Steam Days Remembered III

Strathwood

Southern Steam Days Remembered III

Front Cover: Its just two days to go until closure of the branch from Dunton Green to Westerham. Wainwright's H Class, 31518 from 73J Tonbridge, is well decorated to work one of the service trains on 28 October, 1961 seen making the stop just in case any passengers wish to avail themselves of the chance of a ride at Brasted. *Colour Rail*

Strathwood

Southern Steam Days Remembered III

First published 2017
ISBN 1-905276-78-8
ISBN 978-1-905276-78-3

All rights reserved. No part of this book may be reproduced or transmitted in any form or by any means, electronic or mechanical, including photocopying, recording or by any information storage and retrieval system, without written permission from the Publisher in writing.

Copyright Strathwood Publishing 2017

Published by Strathwood Publishing, 9 Boswell Crescent, Inverness, IV2 3ET
Telephone 01463 234004

Printed by Akcent Media

Contents

Preface

Thankful that the first volume in this Steam Days Remembered series was so well received at its launch during the Eastleigh Works Open Day in 2009, the second and third volume released together are perhaps well overdue, after such a wait.

It was planned to release the second volume a number of years ago, so to those of you who have been patiently waiting for its release with kind words of encouragement, I thank you. The release of both this and the third volume at the same time is to commemorate the fact that fifty years have passed since the demise of regular Southern Region steam in the summer of 1967. As a young school boy at the time living close to Feltham my recollections of this final gasp of the dying steam railway are made all the clearer by the wonderful photographs, thankfully recording this era. Not to mention those who were involved, such as my old friend Roger Carrell, and all of those who have taken the time and trouble, to set down on paper some of their wonderful tales and experiences from this sadly missed time.

Roger and myself made our acquaintance over thirty years ago on the other side of the world from our beloved Southern Region in Western Australia. Through the wonders of email we remain in touch to this day within a close group of friends across the globe who share a passion for British Railways steam.

We will all have our favourites from the past, I hope you will enjoy this compilation and we must also thank the foresight of the photographers and the kindness of those who have allowed their work to be seen and appreciated by a wider audience.

Kevin Derrick
Inverness 2017

Below: The end of steam is very close in this view from the early summer of 1967 at Waterloo with a shabby looking Standard Class 4MT acting as this mornings station pilot amongst the changing liveries of the day. *Rail Online*

Introduction - The Day of the 'Hush Hush' Train

It was a glorious summer Sunday morning in 1964 when Ron Rood and I booked on as 07:00 'spare' at Basing' Loco on one of our rest days. (We always worked Rest Days to boost our income!). We were just settling in to make a can of tea and get the cards out when our Running Foreman, Jim Wilkes, poked his head through the hatch and asked if we'd seen the latest alterations to the duty roster.

A check of the roster revealed that Ron and I were now booked 'Pass' (as passenger) to Eastleigh Loco, prepare our own engine, run light to So'ton New Docks and convey a 'SPL' train to Waterloo. Thence run light to Nine Elms Loco, dispose and home 'Pass'. So, with some mutterings, we gathered our belongings and walked over to the Down Local platform to catch a Hampshire Diesel to Eastleigh (a regular conveyer on the Reading to Southampton Terminus service in those days).

On arrival at Eastleigh Loco, we were given 34006 Bude, an Unmodified Bulleid Pacific, to prepare. That done, we made a can of tea and proceeded to the exit dummy

Thankfully this one of the named Standard Class 5MTs went to Woodham's yard in Barry and has survived. Although sights like this of 73082 Camelot in Southampton's once extensive rail network within the docks once more are highly unlikely. *Colour Rail*

and, without a word from me on the phone, the South Box let us out and sent us merrily on our way, tender first, towards Southampton.

We cautiously took the curve at Northam, ran through Central then Millbrook to find a pilotman awaiting us as we entered the Docks. He conducted us onto our train - a Mk1 BSK festooned with clip-on aerials, followed by three bogie PLVs, each one padlocked to the hilt. No need to wonder what was in those, this being a regular berthing for Union Castle ships.

I jumped down to couple-up and remove my boards (headcode discs) thence to the front of the loco to remove my tail lamp and placed my boards - one at the top and one at bottom right for Waterloo. I then returned to the cab, grabbed my coal pick and clambered up the front of the tender to trim my coal for the journey. Suddenly, as I was wielding my pick, the ground all around me became filled with anxious faces from six uniformed bobbies and two plain clothed detectives, each saying nothing but watching me intently. It took the guard, who had just given Ron our train particulars, to explain that I was just doing my job!

We got 'right-away' about 10:00 and 'Bude' was an easy steamer; pity I never got her on the 17:09 Down from Waterloo each time! There were no sleepers placed across the track or outlaws hiding beside the line anywhere as we chattered our way up the bank towards Roundwood, thence over Battledown, through our home town, and onto the easy gradients towards London.

In fact, the trip was an absolute doddle - with only four on and just maintaining the easy schedule at 60mph, it was one of those perfect occasions that enginemen often dream about but seldom experience with reduced maintenance, etc… As we passed Fleet, I was putting on another round of coal onto what was a perfectly shaped fire when Ron called out that I won't need to do much more - 'She' was quite happy and using very little steam at this pace while in 5% reverse cut-off!

We had been given a clear road right through and the London suburbs were no exception. It occurred to me that being a Sunday there would have been a lot of lineside spotters and photographers around, such that, bandits robbing a gold train without witnesses was virtually impossible!

We sailed into Platform 11 at Waterloo right time and were met by an army of bobbies - (you'd think we had conveyed Her Majesty. the Queen!) - plus black vans in the taxiway! I hopped down and walked to the front to remove my lower disc and replace it with a tail lamp, thence to the rear to uncouple and place my board at bottom right (as viewed from the cab) for Nine Elms Loco. Ron then edged the loco forward to line-up with the column for water.

A visit to Nine Elms on 12 November, 1961 rewards us with a view of 35014 Nederland Line still with her original rebuilt tender and early emblem dating from 1956. *Colour Rail*

Another view of 35014 Nederland Line on shed at Nine Elms a few years later on 10 September, 1966 sees the engine with a different tender as it is ready to head to Waterloo to depart with today's 16:35 Royal Wessex. *Strathwood Library Collection*

An interesting and short lived paint scheme for the tender adorns 35020 Bibby Line in the late spring of 1956 at Nine Elms. *Colour Rail*

It was at this juncture that we were surprised to be approached by a pair of Nine Elms men who stated that they'd been 'spare' and as we hadn't taken 'PN' (physical needs) since booking on, and were going to be trapped at the hydraulics for at least an hour or so during unloading, they'd been sent to relieve us and send us home to Basing' 'Pass'! So we thanked them, collected our belongings and beat a hasty retreat in the direction of the staff canteen which is situated beneath the platforms of the station.

Waterloo station is built upon a (very wide) viaduct which slopes gradually downhill from platform ramps to the generous concourse and anyone who has ventured down there will agree that it resembles a sinister Victorian underworld... with strange odours to match! We entered the spacious canteen, got our free cuppa and sat down to devour our sandwiches. Being a Sunday, we knew there wasn't a train to Basing' for an hour and a half so there would be plenty of time to relax with a few games of cards.

We arrived back at Basing' around 15:00 and made our way home, each wishing that every turn on the footplate was as significant and cushy as that one was . . . we were booked an 03:15 start on a 'goods' to Salisbury tomorrow morning!

Roger Carrell - West Australia 2017

Branches & Byways

A relic from the era of Stirling and 1878, albeit rebuilt at Ashford Works in May 1894 by Wainwright could still be found at work in the Kent coalfield in 1955, as Class O1, 31258 heads away from Tilmanstone Colliery. *Colour Rail*

The large station at Christ's Hospital was for the benefit of the public school which was established in 1552 as the Blue School. The station here was situated on the mainline to Arundel and Littlehampton, with junction connections to cross country routes to Guildford and Brighton. It is on one of these services from Brighton that Class E4, 32566 arrives off the line via Steyning which would close in 1966. It was examples of the Standard Class 4MT, 2-6-4T that would depose these Billington designed Class E4s from the route. *Colour Rail*

Just two passengers are seen at Reigate on 27 September, 1964 to welcome the arrival of Standard Class 4MT, 80152 with the 09:03 Reading to Redhill. *Strathwood Library Collection*

To connect their lines in Kent with the Great Western Railway at Reading, the former South Eastern & Chatham Railway built their line right across the southern counties, thus crossing what the London & South Western Railway viewed as their territory here at Ash. Where in September 1964, Maunsell Moguls such as N Class, 31405 was still at work from 75B Redhill, before being ousted by the Eastleigh built DEMUs that would soon take over these duties. *Late Norman Browne/Strathwood Library Collection*

Right: One of Bulleid's Class Q1s, 33032 from 73J Tonbridge is perhaps unlikely power for the branch set at Allhallows-on-Sea in April, 1960 as the crew make ready for the return along the branch to Gravesend. *Colour Rail*

Today's branch train for Hawkhurst has one of 73C Hither Green's Class C 0-6-0s in charge, as they set off from Paddock Wood in 1955. This 11½ mile long branch was opened in 1893, and passed through the picturesque Kentish hopfields. Sadly the branch was destined to close on 12 June 1961.
Dave Cobbe Collection/Rail Photoprints

Opposite: The first station along the branch was here at Horsemonden, seen in the last few weeks before closure as enthusiasts took their chance for a visit and to grab some photographs for posterity, even in the rain as here on 27 May, 1961 with H Class 31324 with a push pull set now making up the train.
Colour Rail

Opposite: More of these converted push pull sets from 1959, firstly with another H Class, 31518 alongside its home shed at Tunbridge Wells West.
Strathwood Library Collection

In July 1963 it is the turn of one of Tunbridge Wells West's Class M7s to head another of these push pull sets near Groombridge.
Dave Cobbe Collection/Rail Photoprints

The delightful country station at Rowfant was a popular spot for photographers up until its closure on 2 January, 1967. Seen from the angle opposite with H Class 31161 propelling another of these push pull sets in the direction of Three Bridges, we can see why. However, when viewed from the other side as here with classmate 31005 propelling the other way towards East Grinstead on 10 June 1962, we can glimpse the unsightly oil depot situated in the goods yard here. *Colour Rail*

Yet another H Class and push pull set combination is captured firstly on 31 May 1963 drawing to halt at Grange Road whilst bound for Three Bridges with the fireman in charge on the footplate. Then the same locomotive is seen waiting patiently at the high level station at East Grinstead on 19 August, 1962 with a connecting bus service. *Both: Colour Rail*

Certainly busier with its rush hour services was the service from Clapham Junction to here at Kensington Olympia, although definitely less scenic for fans of country branch lines. It was just weeks away from seeing any steam activity when photographed on the morning of 26 May, 1967 as Ivatt Class 2MT 41298 will head the 08:31 up the junction.

Ian Turnbull/Rail Photoprints

Passengers and station staff at North Camp are pleased to see the arrival of N Class, 31405 as it arrives with the 13:16 Ash to Reading on 12 September 1964. At this point this Maunsell Mogul was allocated to 75B Redhill, but would remain a regular here once transferred to 70C Guildford from January, 1965 until withdrawn in June 1966.
Late Norman Browne/Strathwood Library Collection

Much of the variety of classes once seen at North Camp, such as Class T9, 30732 in April 1959 would gradually disappear during the early 1960s. *Colour Rail*

Of course it would not just be ex London & South Western Railway locomotives that would succumb during the 1960s. Even with more modern motive power and the likes of Bournemouth's Standard Class 3MT, 82026 heading yet another of those rebuilt push-pull sets away from West Moors on 1 May 1964 would not stop this station from closure that year. *Colour Rail*

These rebuilt push pull sets made up from Maunsell mainline stock were just a stop gap to allow the Southern Region to phase out wooden bodied stock, whilst awaiting DEMU replacements for steam. They appeared all over the region's surviving branches briefly, as here with Class M7, 30052 firstly at Wareham where the Swanage branch met the London & South Western Railway's mainline. Then once more at Lymington Pier with the 07:20 to Brockenhurst on 1 May, 1963.
Colour Rail & Strathwood Library Collection

Staying at Lymington Pier which connected with steamers to the Isle of Wight, we see another Class M7, 30254 in push pull service on 31 May, 1963. On 25 March 1967, this branch attracted enthusiasts with the Manchester Rail Travel Society's special which employed Standard Class 4MT, 80151 for this leg of their Hants & Dorset Branch Flyer. It was not all doom and gloom for branch lines as this line was electrified a few months later in July.
Strathwood Library Collection & Peter Simmonds

Lots of steam activity on the branch with Class M7, 30129 at Lymington Town with the 10:18 for the pier on 1 June 1963, as another can be glimpsed at the head of the empty push pull set 611 which has another coach augmenting the formation today. Cameras and onlookers a plenty at Weymouth in Southern steam's last year 1967 as Ivatt Class 2MT, 41298 picks its way through what would be today's classic cars.
Strathwood Library Collection & Colour Rail

Waterloo Sunset

Passengers look relaxed as they make their way through Waterloo's main concourse at the former London & South Western Railway's terminal side of this sprawling station during 1964. Whilst outside in the sunshine away down at the platform ends, a little peace and quiet could be found as long as the sounds percolating from 34064 Fighter Command and Standard Class 4MT 80143 don't disturb. *Strathwood Library Collection*

Left and opposite: Standing alongside one of the Portsmouth line's 4-COR units we find 34064 Fighter Command back once again at the country end of the terminus on 5 May 1966, just clearing her cylinders with the drain cocks open for departure. A few minutes earlier as another driver considered how his run might be this morning onboard 34018 Axminster in an adjacent platform road. *Bill Wright*

As the departures of pre-grouping types such as Classes M7s and E4s quickened in the early 1960s, for a short while ex GWR Panniers could be seen alongside them as station pilots. In turn these duties came into the hands of Ivatt Class 2MTs and Standard Class 3MTs and as here on Saturday 11 March, 1967 with Class 4MTs towards the end. *Strathwood Library Collection*

Opposite: Even on a cold winter's day such as 30 December, 1966 young lads in shorts could be found observing the movements of 34019 Bideford and another Class 4MT, 80154. *Late John Green*

One of the then new second production batch of Electro-Diesels waits alongside as enthusiasts capture the departure of 34019 Bideford and 34023 Blackmore Vale on the first leg of this special as far as Fareham on 16 October, 1966. Just compare opposite how filthy Bideford became in the following couple of months. *George Woods*

The stock for this LCGB run special had been brought up from Clapham Junction by 34052 now sadly minus its Lord Dowding nameplates, as we see the Pacific pulling up at the platform end having shoved the special out, against the incline and the reverse curves. *George Woods*

On 4 June 1966 Standard Class 5MT, 73093 in a filthy state over its green livery await's the off alongside another sadly anonymous Class 4MT on pilot duties, with just over a year to go for regular steam at Waterloo.
Strathwood Library Collection

Preservation Beckons

Thankfully both the locomotive and the line survive today, as we see 92220 Evening Star far from stretching itself on the Mid Hants Watercress Line near Alton, on the Southern Counties Touring Society's, Farewell to Steam tour on 20 September 1964. Ropley still enjoyed a daily passenger service albeit with DEMUs on 1 May, 1966. However the route was often used to divert services off the Bournemouth line during electrification works, such as here with 34019 Bideford approaching with the 16:30 Waterloo to Weymouth express. *Strathwood Library Collection & Colour Rail*

The remaining platform at Ropley is crowded on 18 September 1960 as tour participants seize their chance to stretch their legs and grab a shot of L Class, 31768 on this leg of their special. *Rail Online*

Left and opposite: The local stopping DEMU waits at Medstead & Four Mark for 34002 Salisbury to clear the single line with another diverted express on 1 May, 1966. On the same day fellow enthusiasts enjoy the sights and sounds of 35008 Orient Line passing the bluebells on Medstead Bank. *Colour Rail*

Again enthusiasts hang from the windows as Class S15, 30837 pulls through Arlesford on 9 January, 1966. Another location that would become a preservation home for Southern steam would be Swanage. However, there can not have been any thoughts of that on 30 July, 1961 as Class M7, 30057 was engaged in a little shunting. The yard still looks busy with carriages and motor coaches for holiday makers, along with a British Railways Bedford lorry for local goods work. *Both: Colour Rail*

Perhaps inevitably the stock provided for the RCTS Farewell to Southern Steam tour, on 18 June 1967 with just a fortnight to go before the end of steam, should be in the new corporate livery. It was the task of Class 4MT, 80146 to lead the tour back from here at Swanage to the mainline at Wareham with 34089 602 Squadron at the rear of the train. On 11 April 1964, Swanage was host to Class M7, 30053. When it was withdrawn a few weeks later, who could have thought it would then spend twenty years in the USA, before finding its way back here to a preserved railway in 1992?
Colour Rail & Strathwood Library Collection

The venerable Class A1X Terriers have long been associated with the former Colonel Stephens instigated Kent & East Sussex Railway. Built as No. 70 Poplar, this locomotive entered revenue earning service on 4 December 1872. For nearly 30 years it worked suburban trains in the London area. By the turn of the century the Terriers were becoming too small for the many duties they had handled so well, and the LB&SCR decided to reduce their numbers by scrapping. It was quickly discovered, however, that they had a considerable potential on the second hand market. Thus No. 70 was sold to the Rother Valley Railway (later the K&ESR) in May 1901 for £650 and with 664,108 miles to its credit. Brighton Works repainted the locomotive in the blue livery of its new owners and fitted vacuum brakes. As No. 3 Bodiam it well served the K&ESR until 1931 when it was withdrawn together with the line's second Terrier, No. 5 Rolvenden (ex-LB & SCR No 671 Wapping) which had been purchased in 1905. The pair languished rusting on a grassy siding at Rolvenden until, in 1932/33, Rolvenden was cannibalised and various parts used to reconstruct Bodiam and restore it to working order. The name plates were removed at this stage but fortunately survived. In February 1943 its boiler was condemned and one of the A1X pattern, bought from the Southern Railway for £725, was fitted at the Southern Railway's St. Leonards Depot. After nationalisation Bodiam was taken into BR Southern Region stock as No. 32670, although it continued to work the K&ESR, first remaining at Rolvenden and then at St. Leonards. Later, it moved westwards to work the Hayling Island branch. No. 32670 was withdrawn after that branch's closure in November 1963. Once again the locomotive was saved from the scrapheap.
Strathwood Library Collection

Opposite: Credited as being the first privately preserved standard gauge steam locomotive within the United Kingdom, is the ex Great Northern Railway Class J52, 1247 when it was bought out of service from British Railways in May 1959 running as 68846. Here we find it appearing on another first in preservation on the Bluebell Railway, whose early volunteers ensured this would become the first standard gauge preserved line in the country. The now restored Class J52, waits at Horsted Keynes having just arrived from London Bridge with the Bluebell Railway Preservation Society's own Blue Belle Special 1 April 1962. *Gerald T. Robinson*

Southern Belles

Just over three miles into its one hundred and ten mile journey to Bournemouth West from Waterloo in August 1959, 35014 Nederland Line will now be able to pick up speed once clear of Clapham Junction.
Late Norman Browne/Strathwood Library Collection

In August 1965 a Standard Class 4MT Mogul sets off tender first from the sidings at Clapham Junction and heads for Waterloo with the empty stock for today's down Bournemouth Belle. Thoughtfully to try and blend in with the Pullman cars, a Western Region chocolate & cream liveried full brake has been drafted into the formation to bring more luggage capacity during the summer timetable. *Robert Western*

Just over two miles past Basingstoke lies Worting Junction where the Salisbury and West of England line diverges from the Bournemouth route. In 1955, we see 35011 General Steam Navigation heading for the Dorset coast with this morning's Bournemouth Belle. The head codes are set the same in our next view but sadly the name boards have been dispensed with by 15 May, 1965 when we see 34021 Dartmoor on the same working at Hook.
Colour Rail & Peter Coton

For a short period passengers on this prestige service could enjoy 70A Nine Elms allocated Britannia, 70009 Alfred the Great as their motive power. Seen here at Branksome on 21 July 1951, it only worked from Nine Elms for four months before moving to 32A Norwich that October. One of the other equally famous Belles from this era was the all electric service to Brighton, with two of the three five-car sets led by 3052 making up this working on 15 September, 1963 as they rush through East Croydon on their way from Victoria to the Sussex seaside. *Colour Rail & Rail Online*

Opposite and right: From a vantage point by the entrance to Clayton Tunnel on 7 October 1962 we see 5-BEL set number 3053 leading this ten coach formation, the gathered cameramen are here to see Schools Class 30925 Cheltenham which is following with a special also bound for Brighton. A very rare colour view of the short-lived Kentish Belle which also was known as the Thanet Belle previously, seen here at Bromley in 1952, its last year of running, the engine in charge today is 34063 229 Squadron. **Colour Rail**

Also dressed in one of the early experimental liveries is 34011 Tavistock complete with those dramatic side name boards at Exmouth Junction shed in June 1949. This Devon Belle service was still relatively new, having been launched by the Southern Railway on 16 June 1947. It was a popular all Pullman service from Waterloo to Ilfracombe and Plymouth, scheduled to leave Waterloo behind a Merchant Navy, handing over to a Light Pacific at Exeter Central. This was a summer timetable only service, running at first on weekends only. **Colour Rail**

Above: One of the notable features and attractions to luxury seeking Pullman service passengers was the use of the Devon Belle observation cars, seen at Honiton in 1947 and a year later being turned at Ilfracombe.
Strathwood Library Collection

Bottom right: In the first few months of running the Devon Belle we find 21C13 Blue Funnel on a down working at Basingstoke in September 1947.
Colour Rail

This often well patronised service at a time when everyone wanted to get away for their summer holidays after many long years of war, as air travel was still very expensive and car ownership a rarity, it was a real treat to travel in style on the Devon Belle. In August 1947, the driver of 21C11 General Steam Navigation holds back his steed until they are clear of Clapham Junction, and he can open her up a bit. *Colour Rail*

The interior view of one of the two Devon Belle observation cars, albeit after they were transferred to Scotland for use of the West Highland line, losing their Pullman livery in the process to blend in with then standard maroon coach livery at the end of the 1954 summer timetable, and the Devon Belle was no more. *Late Vincent Heckford/Strathwood*

The southern was not new to changing tastes and dictates in colour schemes, as both Maunsell and Bulleid had introduced a number a livery changes in their times, some of course brought about by wartime measures. In the early summer of 1951, 35020 Bibby Line was captured standing outside Eastleigh Works after a light intermediate overhaul, and a touch up to her blue livery. This combination at Bournemouth in 1949, was clearly applied very early in 1948, as Urie designed King Arthur 30736 Excalibur wears a crossover livery with her new British Railways number. *Both: Colour Rail*

Combinations at Branksome in July 1951, whilst the Black Five is in unlined black and lettered British Railways, the Drummond Class S11, 30403 retains its Southern unlined black but has acquired its new number on both its cabsides and smoke box. In a couple of months time during September it will be withdrawn anyway, the three car rake of coaches also appear to be still in their Southern Railway guise, behind the single Maunsell coach. Also still proudly displaying its heritage at Bournemouth two summers earlier in August 1949, was Class E1 2112 which never lasted long enough to be adorned with its British Railways number as 32112, being withdrawn in December 1949. *Both: Colour Rail*

The once showpiece pride of the Southern Railway, 21C1 Channel Packet was very much overdue a visit to Eastleigh Works when recorded at Exmouth Junction in June 1949. This would take place during September and October the same year, with 35001 Channel Packet being released in the then new blue livery with straw lining and a large British Railways crest. The distinctive early cab design would not be modified until late 1950. *Colour Rail*

Standing majestically at Stewarts Lane we find 35027 Port Line in the blue livery she carried from April 1950 until October 1953, when she went green again. *Colour Rail*

Beauty and the beast perhaps, with Billington's Class H2 Atlantic design, 2421 South Foreland resplendent in Southern Railway colours outside her home shed at Newhaven in 1947. She would be renumbered as 32421 in May 1949 and painted into unlined black without an emblem on her tender initially. As for the beast, we apologise as there are only two known colour shots of Bulleid's Leader 36001, this being the most interesting of it being painted in the works yard at Eastleigh in June 1948. *Both: Colour Rail*

Opposite: Exhibiting a trial colour scheme at Eastleigh Works in early 1949, we find 35024 East Asiatic Company which only lasted a short while, a matter of weeks. *Colour Rail*

Above: Just like 35024 opposite it is probable that the British Railways emblem on 34090 Sir Eustace Missenden, Southern Railway was hand painted as it was released new to traffic the same month. Here it is photographed at Nine Elms in February 1949, having just been named by its namesake the former head of the Southern Railway on 15 February at Waterloo. *Colour Rail*

Fellow light Pacific 34016 Bodmin had been new as 21C116 on 28 November 1945, but when seen ex works at Eastleigh in March 1948 it had just been repainted but kept its old number with an s added, proper renumbering took place early in July with the locomotive carrying this colour scheme until adopting the then standard British Railways green livery in January 1950. *Colour Rail*

The rusty wheels suggests that Urie designed King Arthur Class, 30742 Camelot has been inactive recently when recorded at Eastleigh in May 1950. The malachite green livery dates back to an overhaul in later Southern Railway days during 1946, with the painters adopting their familiar sunshine style of numbering and lettering to proclaim the new nationalised railway in October 1948. A similar treatment befell the former Royal engine, Class T9, 30119 seen on shed at 71C Dorchester on 26 April, 1952. Unique as the only green Class T9 in any form of British Railways livery, this elegant locomotive was withdrawn on 31 December 1952, and cut up within Ashford Works during July the following year. *Both: Colour Rail*

Opposite: A newly built tender for a Bulleid Light Pacific stands alongside Terrier 377S with its attractive rendition of a former LBSCR livery as the Brighton Works pilot in late 1947. It would become DS377 in this livery in the following year, being finally renumbered and painted into lined black as 32635 in May 1959. *Colour Rail*

The adoption of the new identity for Class 0298, 30587 when renumbered during July 1948 took up this style. Now ready for a works visit here at Eastleigh in 1954 it will be sent out with then standard smaller version of the early British Railways emblem. *Colour Rail*

Several of Drummond's Class M7s were painted in versions of the Southern Railway's green liveries at the creation of British Railways in 1948. Whilst the new standard livery for overhauls and repaints for the first nine locomotives overhauled in 1948, saw them released in unlined black, for some they would adopt this style when renumbered as modelled by 30244, until they too went for overhaul and would all then adopt the familiar standard mixed traffic livery of lined black thereafter. *Strathwood Library Collection*

The variations and range of liveries was extensive for the first few years of the newly nationalised railway, here are some Southern Region examples; 30864 Sir Martin Frobisher at Southampton in July 1948. Then two Schools Class locomotives, 30913 Christ's Hospital at Redhill in 1949, and 900 Eton just before renumbering in May 1948 at Cannon Street, and opposite a close up this time of Class S11 30403 at Bournemouth in the summer of 1951.

Colour Rail & Strathwood Library Collection

More uncertainty over what exactly the new livery standards should be is exhibited at Eastleigh with Class T9, 30726 in the spring of 1949 with a backdrop of a King Arthur Class tender still in Southern guise. Whilst another King Arthur heads back into traffic after overhaul at Eastleigh at the same time repainted into an anonymous version of Southern colours with new numbering as 30774 Sir Gaheris. *Both: Colour Rail*

Having been in a similar malachite green but without any sunshine yellow lining when new on 11 December 1948, by the spring of 1950, 35027 Port Line had been given this striking blue livery. We see the Merchant Navy class locomotive fully dressed for working this most prestigious train at Victoria in 1952. *Colour Rail*

This example of the Merchant Navy Class was new into traffic on 4 December, 1948 as 35026 in unlined Malachite Green, naming as Lamport & Holt Line would not take place until 15 January 1951, when it was named together with 35028 Clan Line in a ceremony within Southampton Docks. During 1949 it was painted into the then standard livery for the class of lined blue, but now in the mid 1950s it was along with all of her classmates now in the new standard lined green livery as she was dressed for departure with today's down Golden Arrow at Victoria. Also of note is how the background colour of the headboard reflects this new livery too. *Colour Rail*

Opposite: New to traffic on 14 October 1948, 34083 has still to be named as 605 Squadron when seen in malachite green with sunshine yellow lining and dressed with all of the Golden Arrow regalia at Victoria in early 1949. *Colour Rail*

In the more relaxed and security free world of the late 1950s, there is time for a conversation with today's footplate crew onboard 34089 602 Squadron before departure time at 11:00 sharp. The ostentatious golden side arrows were of course different between the original Bulleid Pacifics and the rebuilds. With 34100 Appledore and 34101 Hartland which is seen here on departure from Victoria on 31 March 1961, both having fixing studs added to their smoke deflectors by Stewarts Lane for this duty. *Robin Brown Collection & Frank Hornby*

Likewise both 70004 William Shakespeare and 70014 Iron Duke, seen here at Stewarts Lane and allocated to the Golden Arrow duty rosters from 1951 until early 1958, also carried fixing studs on their smoke deflectors as here in 1957. Stewarts Lane were very proud of their prestige service and always turned out the motive power in a bulled up condition as witnessed by 35027 Port Line during 1954 rolling through Brixton. *Strathwood Library Collection*

Opposite: The last of the Merchant Navy class to be rebuilt would be 35028 Clan Line seen here approaching Shortlands Junction in September 1958. The following year would see it rebuilt, but for now complete with unmodified tender it is the only one of her class to get the later crest in this condition. *Dave Cobbe Collection/Rail Photoprints*

Above and left: On the down Golden Arrow near Paddock Wood in 1960 we find the newly rebuilt 34088 213 Squadron whilst 34085 501 Squadron is set to rattle the rafters as it passes the station here on 15 August, 1959. *Both: Colour Rail*

Opposite and left: Another view of the last unrebuilt Merchant Navy, 35028 Clan Line from 1959 as she makes a sturdy sight at Abbotscliffe between the tunnels near the foreshore. In charge once again is 34085 501 Squadron, this time in May 1959 at Dover. *Both: Colour Rail*

Two years later and we return to Dover to witness 34100 Appledore in its heyday being turned on the shed's turntable and being made ready to work the return Golden Arrow back to London's Victoria station, hopefully the boat will have berthed on time on 29 May, 1961. *Gerald T. Robinson*

87

Bulleid Nameplate Glory

34001 Exeter, 34004 Yeovil, 34006 Bude, 34008 Padstow & 34015 Exmouth.
Strathwood Library Collection

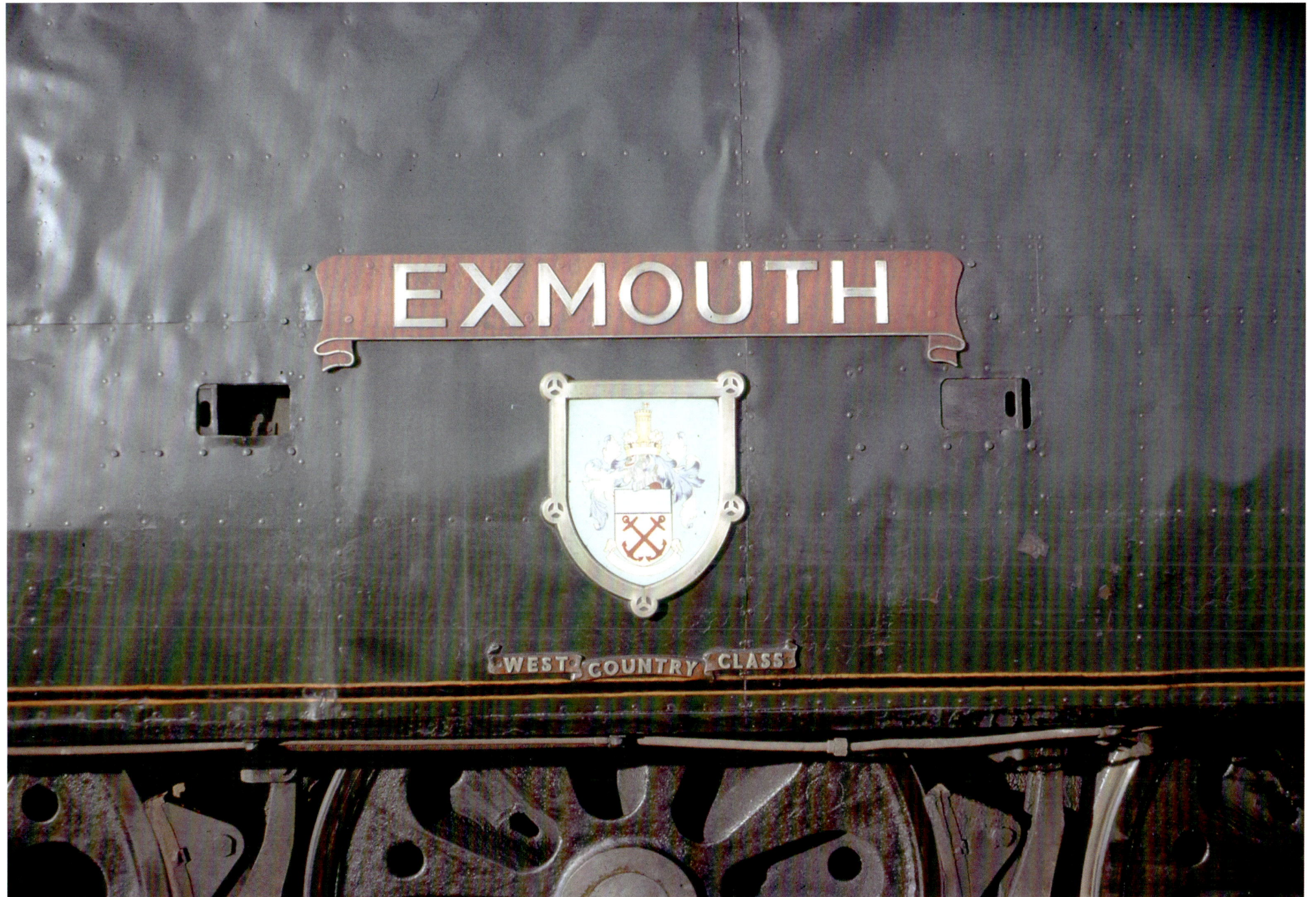

35027 Port Line, 34050 Royal Observer Corps, 34066 Spitfire, 34089 602 Squadron, 34090 Sir Eustace Missenden Southern Railway, 34012 Launceston, 34104 Bere Alston, 34013 Okehampton, 35029 Ellerman Lines & 34018 Axminster. *Strathwood Library Collection*

Oh Dear!

It looks like 34061 73 Squadron has endured a lagging fire from all of the oil splashing about from those chain driven valves, from her appearance outside Eastleigh Works in September 1962. She would return to service in early November after repairs in the works, but she would be withdrawn on 16 August, 1964 and cut up by the end of the following winter by Messrs Woods at Queenborough on the Isle of Sheppey. On 20 July 1952, 30854 Howard of Effingham came to grief near Shawford. Being beyond the range of cranes, the embankment had to be excavated and a recovery track laid to drag it back up to track level. After a brief visit to the nearby Eastleigh Works the Lord Nelson Class locomotive was back in traffic once more on 11 September. *Both: Colour Rail*

Opposite and below: Two separate incidents at Whitchurch in Hampshire, firstly with Standard Class 4MT, 76017 which had been working an early morning Banbury to Southampton freight on 23 September, 1954. When it became derailed at the south end of the loop and then nose dived down the steep embankment. Almost unbelievably 76026, another of these Standard Class 4MT Moguls almost went down the same bank too on 12 February 1960, after overrunning signals and being caught by the trap points.
Both: Colour Rail

In 1958, Standard Class 5MT, 73111 soon to carry the name King Uther, but for today has to suffer the indignity of being off the road at Millbrook. This thankfully minor mishap was caused by a faulty point motor moving the points under the train. **Colour Rail**

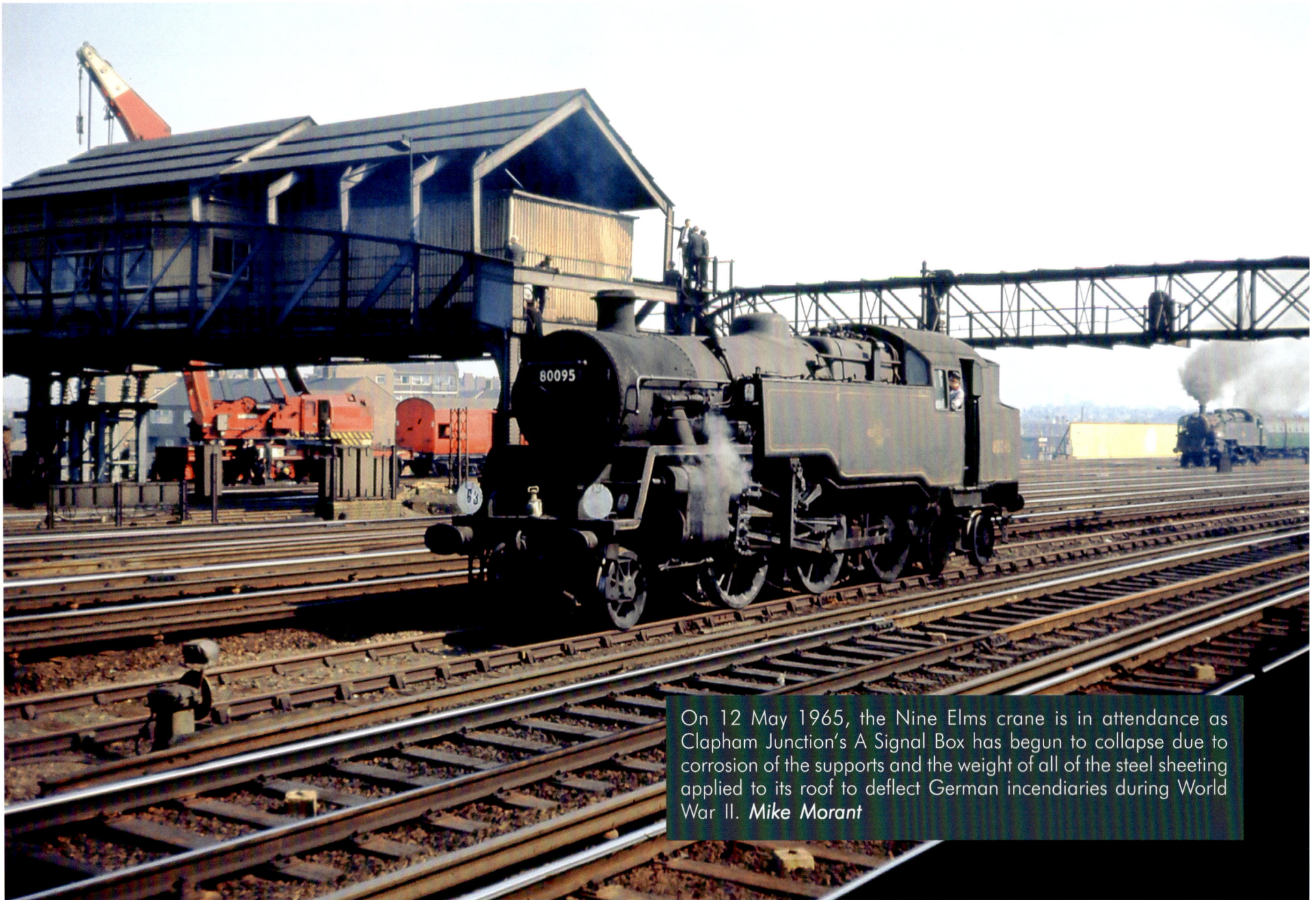

On 12 May 1965, the Nine Elms crane is in attendance as Clapham Junction's A Signal Box has begun to collapse due to corrosion of the supports and the weight of all of the steel sheeting applied to its roof to deflect German incendiaries during World War II. *Mike Morant*

Not incendiaries, but the effects of another lagging fire have befallen 34049 Anti-Aircraft Command as it awaits entry to Eastleigh Works in 1957. This was the only Battle of Britain class member to carry a red backed oval crest, drawn from the Army regiment whose badge is of a longbow being fired upwards against a red background. *Colour Rail*

Shed Panoramas

Diesels are starting to outnumber steam locomotives in this view of Basingstoke shed in early 1966. Originally coded as 70D it was demoted as a stabling point to Eastleigh which adopted this shed code as of 29 September 1963. Perhaps inevitably then the shed here would close upon the last day of Southern Region steam 9 July 1967. The appearance of the wooden shed part of 72E Barnstaple Junction in May 1963, leaves a little to be desired. On 9 September the same year it would be ceded to the Western Region and given the new code of 83F, closing on 15 September a year later.
Both: Strathwood Library Collection

A splendid view from the coaling tower at 70B Feltham across to the once expansive hump yards in 1961, as can be seen the diesel shunter invasion has taken place consigning a number of steam duties to history already. Whilst Feltham would close in 1970, across in south east London 73C Hither Green would carry on for some time as a diesel and electric depot. On 13 May 1961 examples of the new traction were on hand alongside W Class 31913 which would find itself based at Feltham for its last few months in traffic in 1964. *Strathwood Library Collection & Rail Online*

In 1847 the London & South Western Railway established an engine shed here at Salisbury, over the years it developed and grew along with the railway. For example the 42 ft. turntable was replaced by one of 55 ft. this in turn was replaced as the size of the locomotives increased to a new 65 ft. one being installed in 1912. On 28 July 1963, 34067 Tangmere was out in the shed yard. The shed layout at Bournemouth incorporated a lifting shed seen to the right as unrebuilt 34086 219 Squadron draws into the station past a shed full of rebuilt Bulleid Pacifics. *Both: **Strathwood Library Collection***

Its Sunday 24 June 1962 and we can see at least fourteen locomotives on shed across the field alongside 72C Yeovil. This would be another Southern shed transferred into the Western Region in September 1963 becoming 83E. This code had previously been for St. Blazey which was promoted to 84B.

Enthusiasts gather at 75A Brighton on 15 September 1963 to enjoy the spectacle of the unique Caledonian Railway Single, 123 and the preserved Drummond T9 on shed for servicing as part of their runs from Victoria to Haywards Heath for the Bluebell Railway. *Rail Online & Colour Rail*

Hayling's Terriers

Opposite: An interesting arrangement of stock for today's 15:05 Havant to Hayling Island gets away towards the island on 27 July 1963, with 36270 complete with spark arrester on its chimney. *Dave Cobbe/Rail Photoprints*

Above: In June 1962, 36278 shows the need for the spark arrester as the pugnacious engines often had to be worked hard on well loaded trains, and the possibility of fires being started on the timber trestles of Langstone Bridge was always of concern. *Colour Rail*

Left: Approaching Havant with the well loaded 17:47 service off the island on 25 June 1961, is 32646 with the fireman catching the cool breeze riding shotgun, to escape the heat of the cramped cab. *Gerald T. Robinson*

Time for conversation as 36278 waits to head back towards Hayling Island from the junction with the mainline here at Havant on 1 June 1963, whilst 36246 waits for release at the other end of the bay platform. *Peter Simmonds*

We catch her in action once again a year later at Havant in October 1963, shortly before the end of the line and her withdrawal. Surplus to the LBSCR she was sold to the LSWR in 1903, becoming 734 in their numbering scheme. Later she was renumbered again as W2, then again as W8 and given the name Freshwater on the Isle of Wight, before a return to the mainland in 1949 as 32646. *Tony Butcher*

Left: One of the regulars on the branch 32646 trundles along nicely near Havant heading for the Langston Bridge and the island on 13 October 1962. She was a real old timer at this point, having been built in 1877 by the LBSCR and given the number 46 and named Newington when new. *Gerald T. Robinson*

There were two small intermediate halts as stations on the line, first stop after departing Havant would be here at Langston, where we see 32661 arriving in 1956. Next would come the rather more temporary looking affair that was North Hayling, where 36246 draws in during 1962 in the hope of some traffic. *Dave Cobbe Collection/Rail Photoprints* *& Strathwood Library Collection*

The branch to Hayling Island was popular on many counts, it was a great location for a day out by the seaside, it was photogenic and of course those cute little Terriers were the only approved locomotives permitted to use the line because of the weight restrictions of Langston Bridge. So it would come as no surprise the farewell special run from London on 3 November 1963, would draw crowds. The special on the branch was top and tailed with 32670 and 32636 where the sun shone for the photostop at Langston in the early afternoon. *Tony Butcher*

Southern Specials

On 8 March 1964, the Southern Counties Touring Society ran their South Western Rambler Railtour from Waterloo via a circuitous route to reach Salisbury behind 70020 Mercury which had come over from 1A Willesden. We see the Britannia Pacific going well here getting away from the Andover Junction stop. Another well patronised tour on 12 March 1967 was entitled The Marquess Goes South West was chased for the day by our cameraman on its long winded journey towards Eastleigh, he caught her in the sunshine here at Leigham Junction. *Strathwood Library Collection & Mike Morant*

Posing for the assembled cameramen and tour participants on shed at Ashford on 12 September 1954, are E Class 31166 and D Class 31737. It was late afternoon and after visiting both the works and the shed members of the RCTS would soon board their Invicta special for the run back to Blackfriars in London. The green livery of Ivatt Class 2MT, 46509 from 1A Willesden has been spruced up here at Clapham Junction for the first leg of a jaunt on both the Southern and Western Region's lines along the Thames Valley in 1965.
Colour Rail & Strathwood Library Collection

Opposite: Another route synonymous with the Terriers was the Kent & East Sussex Railway, where we find 36270 top and tailing with 32662 making a photostop at Tenterden on 11 June 1961. Note the cameraman scrambling on the station roof, he was not alone as at least one other was up there too! Author's warning please don't try it again today.
Strathwood Library Collection

On what would turn out to be a scorching hot day ahead, the preserved Drummond T9 is almost ready to depart from Waterloo on 24 June 1962. Heading for Horsham via Guildford, Cranleigh and Christs Hospital to hand over to 32417, 32503, 32353 for further legs before meeting up once more for a run to London Bridge assisted in part by Class M7, 30055.
Late Vincent Heckford/Strathwood Library Collection

Tours run by the LCGB at this time seemed to favour the term Limited in their title, as we next see L Class, 31768 rolling along the Mid Hants route near Medstead and Four Marks on 18 September 1960. The differing bunker arrangements show up in this view of these two USA tanks heading along the Fawley branch on 19 March 1966, with the LCGB's New Forester Railtour. *Colour Rail & Rail Photoprints*

Among the host of specials run for the benefit of enthusiasts was this interesting duo of the preserved Caledonian Railway Single, 123 and the ex London & South Western Railway Class T9, 120. This colourful pairing are seen going well on the former London Brighton & South Coast Railway's down line at Purley Oaks on 15 September 1963 as they make for Haywards Heath with the celebrated Blue Belle special. Here the Bluebell Railway took over with their own preserved motive power for a run via Ardingley to Horsted Keynes and Sheffield Park. With a return run back to Victoria in the same way later that afternoon. *Mike Morant*

Opposite: Back to the LCGB's rail tour on 18 September, 1960 and to the Fawley branch overlooking the Solent and the vast oil refinery here. This Urie Class H16 was at the time almost a regular here during the classes short spell allocated to Eastleigh. Having brought the tour from Eastleigh via Southampton Central this hefty tank locomotive would return the train back along the branch to Totton, where 30782 Sir Brian would be waiting to take over for the next leg this afternoon. *Rail Online*

Further ex London & South Western Railway activity. Firstly at the electrified branch terminus at Hampton Court on 2 December 1962, where the presence of an inspector keeps everyone on their toes as the duo of Class 0298s are made ready for the run back along the branch to the mainline once more. The other engine involved with this tour was Class H16, 30517 now back once more at 70B Feltham and due for withdrawal after the repeat running of this tour two weeks later, when the two Well Tanks ran bunker to bunker instead. When the LCGB's Surrey Wanderer tour was run on 5 July 1964, ex LSWR locomotives were now in short supply, so this Class M7 seen at Tattenham Corner held sway with 1A Willesden's Class 2MT, 78038 for the day. *Tony Butcher & Dave Southern*

Although working Class S15s could be found in late 1964, all of the original Urie examples were now laid up and withdrawn. Leaving a handful of the Maunsell versions available for tours such as this one on 18 October. The tour had begun on this lovely brisk morning at Waterloo behind 30839 making a short stop at Frimley, before heading for Woking where USA Tank 30064 would take over next for a run through picturesque Baynards, although the famous Dahlias would have gone over by now. *Strathwood Library Collection*

An ASLEF strike had postponed the running of this tour by two days from 12 to 14 June 1955. Although it does not seem to have deterred anyone in this view at Lewes as Brighton Atlantic Class H2 32426 St. Albans Head has its route discs applied for the run over the Bluebell route via Horsted Keynes, albeit a couple of years before the fledgling preservation movement started. *Strathwood Library Collection*

We suspect the gap in the buildings along the quayside here at Weymouth is a reminder of the town's importance during World War Two. On 3 July 1966 we see 41298 one of a number Ivatt Class 2MT 2-6-2Ts in the area, as it threads through the streets on the line to the quay with the LCGB's ill fated Green Arrow Rail Tour past a wonderful selection of what was then everyday motor cars. *Gerald T. Robinson*

Back to the Midhurst Belle on 18 October 1964, where USA Tank 30064 had taken over from 30839 seen previously at Woking. By the time of arrival here at Guildford the crew were anxious to ensure their locomotive was running once more with full tanks before departure towards Stammerham Junction via Baynards and Christs Hospital where Q Class 30530 was on next. *Strathwood Library Collection*

31574

Opposite: Sadly the graceful lines of Wainwright's D Class 4-4-0 design would not last much longer when this view was recorded of 31574 on shed at Ashford in September 1956 as a thunderstorm brews in the Kentish skies above. The following month this example was withdrawn and by the end of the year the class would be extinct, save for 31737 saved for the National Collection. Twenty eight of the class survived into the British Railway's era. Although some had been rebuilt by Maunsell and took on a somewhat different appearance, these original locomotives where perhaps the epitome of Edwardian elegance *Colour Rail*

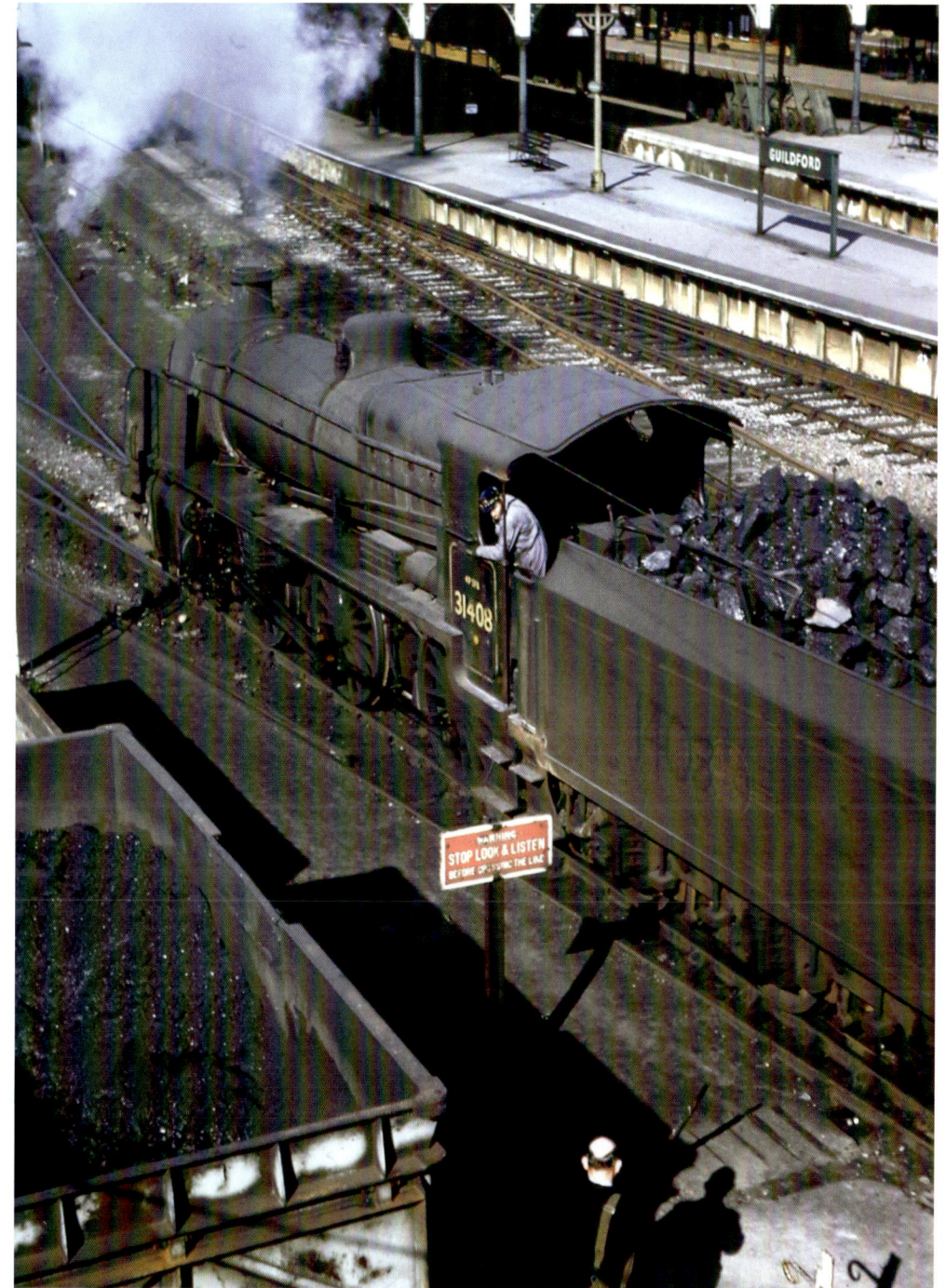

Just over a decade later and even the likes of Maunsell's N Class Moguls were also on their last death throws as here on 8 March 1966 at Guildford. Eighty of these useful locomotives dating from 1917 had been on the books at nationalisation. The first two withdrawals not taking place until 1962, however 1964 would be a bad year for the class as their numbers fell to just twelve examples. Six locomotives hung on until the start of this their final year 1966, with 31408 having just taken on coal, being among the last three withdrawn in September. *Colour Rail*

Perhaps it was fortunate that USA tank, 30072 took over duties as shed pilot at 70C Guildford in February 1963, where its short wheelbase and power would be useful for shunting dead locomotives in the tight confines around the shed's turntable. We see it on duty in 1966, thankfully it was saved for preservation albeit then as it seemed at the unlikely location for a Southern Region engine of Keighley in West Yorkshire. Having just replenished its tender at Guildford's coal stage, 30798 Sir Hectimere is eased towards the turntable roads in June 1962 just days away from being withdrawn.

Win Wall/ Strathwood Library Collection & Colour Rail

The appearance of 30798 Sir Hectimere is quite different a couple of years previously in this view from April 1960 by Basingstoke's coal stage. At this point the Class N15 still carries its original short wheelbase tender. A works visit to Eastleigh that October saw it swapped for the larger tender from the withdrawn 30450 Sir Kay seen seen previously. Sticking at Basingstoke from a viewpoint from the station's platforms we can see 6129 from the former Western Region shed, now 2D Banbury, making its way towards the shed for servicing on 17 July 1964. *Colour Rail & Rail Online*

Two elegant posed shots at Eastleigh, firstly with perhaps the world's most famous steam locomotive in 1964. Then with one of the wide splasher variants of Drummonds T9 Class, 30300 on its home shed from 1951 until being withdrawn in 1961. Sadly for this 4-4-0 it would be scrapped here at Eastleigh within five weeks of being posted as withdrawn. *Strathwood Library Collection*

The dubious privilege of being the last active Maunsell Class S15 fell to 70B Feltham's 30837 early in 1966. It had been previously withdrawn along with the last four surviving classmates in September the previous year. With some care and attention she was made available for the LCGB to run not just one, but two specials with her in January 1966. They ran from Waterloo to here at Eastleigh where we see her on 9 January being prepared for the return run whilst the tour's participants enjoyed a conducted tour of the works. *Tony Butcher*

It looks like Urie Class H16, 30520 also from 70B Feltham has made a visit to the works at Eastleigh in 1961 for some light repairs. Five of these 4-6-2T locomotives were built to work local freight from the then soon to be opened Feltham hump marshalling yard and the new shed built alongside during 1921/2. They first went for a short while whilst new to the shed at nearby Strawberry Hill, until the new shed at Feltham was ready for them. All steam work from Strawberry Hill then transferred across and the old shed was converted to a depot to house the new EMUs being introduced to this part of south west London at this time. *Colour Rail*

Our old friend 35027 Port Line pops up once again awaiting her chance to return back into service at Eastleigh. She was rebuilt into this form here during the late spring of 1957, having run 363,351 miles since entering service in her original form in December 1948. She would be withdrawn from the books in September 1966 whilst allocated to Bournemouth. Thankfully she was purchased by that most famous of Welsh scrap dealers Dai Woodham, who took her into his yard in November of the same year. Here she would stay until leaving for restoration in December 1982. Awaiting her turn to move into the works at Eastleigh in 1954 was 30932 Blundells complete with her high sided tender. This long line alongside the running shed would often have both engines for repairs and for breaking up awaiting their call into the works. *Both: Colour Rail*

A chance to record all three of the surviving Class 0298, Beattie designed 0-4-2WTs at Eastleigh in December 1962 upon their withdrawal was too good to miss. The oldest of this trio was built in 1874, and all three owed their longevity to their ability to deal with tight curves, as such the LSWR sent them from their original duties near London to work the Wenford Bridge china clay line in Cornwall, where we see 30585 standing on Wadebridge shed's turntable on 28 June 1961.
Strathwood Library Collection & Colour Rail

On 3 July 1966 the LCGB ran their Green Arrow Railtour from Waterloo with 34002 Salisbury seen here being turned at Weymouth. Unfortunately the Class V2, 60919 which had come down from Dundee to appear on this tour had failed and was stood at Basingstoke shed at this time whilst the Bulleid's crew set their backs into turning their Pacific. The fireman stands in the tender of 34039 Boscastle on 4 May 1963, as they await their chance to head to the 'Cenotaph' as Nine Elm's large ferro-concrete coaler was sometimes irreverently called. *Tony Butcher & Frank Hornby*

What more appropriate motive power for the Stephenson Locomotive Society's, Stephenson Special from London Bridge to here at Brighton on 23 June 1956 is seen being serviced, although the return leg would be in the hands of K Class 32337, rather than 32329 Stephenson. The piles of ash at Exmouth Junction are comparable alongside 35029 Ellerman Lines in the sunshine here on 30 August 1964. *Strathwood Library Collection & Rail Online*

Up the Links

Tail lamps appear to be fixed both to H Class 31543 at Tonbridge, and the inspection saloon at Fratton in 1963 even though they are both moving forwards as they were photographed. *Both: Colour Rail*

In theory the Engineers' Dept. still retain a claim on the former 30061 back once more among the glamorous ocean liners in Southamton Docks on 6 June 1964, in-spite of being banished to the nearby Redbridge Sleeper Works as DS233 since October 1962. The engineers have possession of the lines around Walton-on-Thames on 1 May 1966, with U Class 31791 engaged on ballast duties in connection with the Bournemouth route's full electrification. *Both: Colour Rail*

The crew of 35028 Clan Line make good use of the hoses provided for filling the cisterns in the carriage toilets to water down their generous coal load, for what looks like a featherweight duty from Weymouth on 5 August 1966. *Colour Rail*

The young looking fireman heeds the words of the master on board Schools Class 30929 Malvern in June 1959 as they have been signalled right away at Paddock Wood.
Dave Cobbe/Rail Photoprints

At Basingstoke on 7 March 1966, the driver shields his eyes against the low winter sunshine as he looks back along his train to see how the passengers and parcels traffic are getting along. Meanwhile his fireman tends to his duties as a couple of budding young enthusiasts perhaps build on their memories of steam engines for the future. *Colour Rail*

Just a few minutes at the platform ends at Waterloo for the crew of 34034 Honiton, as they await their signal to clear the busy station throat light engine, having no doubt assisted out the previous working that had been blocking them in. *Colour Rail*

There are many years of experience of the railway in the face of this driver at Salisbury on 20 March 1966 as there is just time for a few words at the platform ends before taking 34089 602 Squadron forward once more. We conclude for now with one of the favourites of ex-fireman Roger Carrell, as

73082 Camelot makes brisk work of this interesting working at Micheldever which includes a green liveried ex-Pullman car in the rake during May 1962. *Gilroy A. Kerr & Colour Rail*

Also of interest from Strathwood to collect

London Midland Steam Days Remembered
London Midland Steam Days Remembered II
Eastern Steam Days Remembered
Western Steam Days Remembered
Scottish Steam Days Remembered

Looking back at English Electric Locomotives
Looking back at Warships
Looking back at Class 50 Locomotives
Looking back at Class 33 Locomotives

Sixties Diesel & Electric Days Remembered
Sixties Diesel & Electric Days Remembered III
Sixties Diesel & Electric Days Remembered IV
Sixties Diesel & Electric Days Remembered V

Published by Strathwood, 9 Boswell Crescent,
Inverness, IV2 3ET. Tel 01463 234004
www.strathwood.co.uk

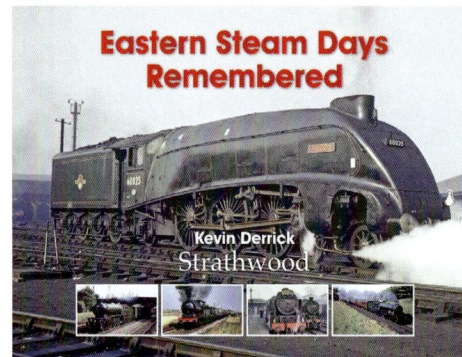

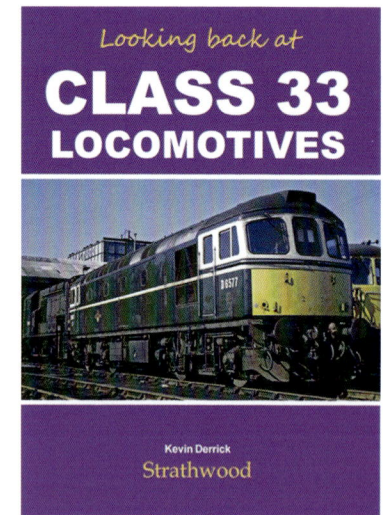

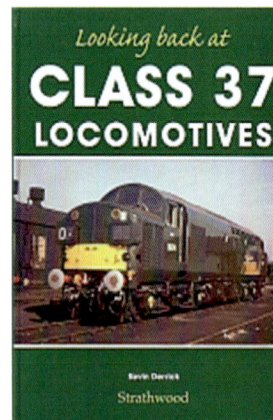

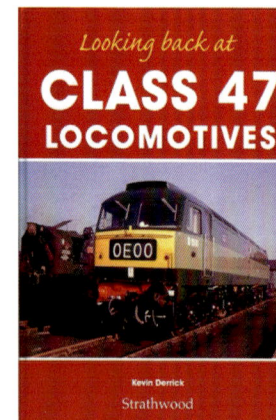